"Good Job"

INTRODUCTION

This book is about taking risks, following your passion, and not being afraid to go after your dreams.

It is dedicated to students and recent graduates who are just starting their careers and trying to figure it out; adults who are stuck in dead-end 9-to-5 jobs, but are too scared to do anything else; and anyone else who just wants to do more and *be* more.

I've been fortunate—or I should say, blessed—to be able to pursue my passion of being a journalist. I want to inspire others to do the same.

I grew up in Baton Rouge, La. in a working-class family. I was the first in my family to graduate from college. I always wanted more than just a J-O-B.

After graduating from Southern University, I went for it. I moved hundreds of miles away from home to work as a paid intern at the *Grand Rapids Press* in Grand Rapids, Mich. I was living my dream. That was followed by other stints in Muskegon, Mich.; Chicago; Houston; Beaumont, Texas; and now my hometown of Baton Rouge.

"Good Job"

My work has been featured in the *Grand Rapids Press, Muskegon Chronicle*, *JET*, *Time*, *People*, *Emerge,* the *Houston Chronicle*, and *O The Oprah Magazine*. I've worked in nearly every facet of media—newspapers, magazines, public relations, television, and digital media. I like to tell people, "I was multimedia before multimedia was cool." In addition, I've also been a successful entrepreneur, working as a freelance writer and public relations consultant.

I've learned many lessons along the way that I'd like to share with you. I want to help motivate you to get off your couch and start living your dreams. I want to help you get over the fear that is keeping you stuck in that job that you stopped enjoying a long time ago—if you ever did. I want to inspire you to take risks and get out of your comfort zone.

In Louisiana, people are always saying things like, "You got that *good job* down at the TV station" or "You got that *good job* at the plant." But as my friend Maureen once told me, "It's not a good job if it's not a good job for YOU."

I want you to have the job or career that you really enjoy—one that gets you excited to get up in the morning and something to which you can look forward. I want you to have a career that's not just paying the bills, but one

"Good Job"

where you feel a connection—where you really feel, "This is where I belong." I want you to have a career that you are passionate about. I've done it. I know you can do it too. I'm not saying it's easy, but I know for a fact that it's well worth the effort.

In this book, you will learn:

- **How to move forward, despite the fear**
- **The importance of having the right attitude and making the right decision**
- **How to develop a plan to get what you want**
- **The art of conducting an informational interview and networking**
- **The rewards of stepping out on faith.**

I'll walk you through my journey to help you navigate yours. Let's enjoy the ride.

ACKNOWLEDGEMENTS

This book is dedicated to all the people who have gone before me and fought the battles that needed to be fought in order for us to enjoy our freedoms—one of which is pursuing a career that you enjoy. It is also dedicated to all those who are continuing to fight for justice and equality.

"Good Job"

And it's dedicated to my beloved *alma mater,* Southern University. Thanks for opening doors, creating opportunities, and showing me the possibilities.

I want to thank my parents, godparents, goddaughter, my siblings, nieces, nephews and the rest of my extended family and friends for all their love and support. Thanks also to my colleagues and mentors who have helped shape my career along the way. I am also very grateful to my friend and editor Maureen Jenkins.

Finally, I want to congratulate those who are taking risks every day and stepping out of their comfort zones to follow their dreams. You rock!

"Good Job"

TABLE OF CONTENTS

CHAPTER 1	No More Tears (Moving Forward Despite the Fear)
CHAPTER 2	The Right Attitude
CHAPTER 3	The Right Place at the Right Time
CHAPTER 4	Making the Right Decision
CHAPTER 5	Living in the Big City
CHAPTER 6	Changing Course
CHAPTER 7	Corporate America
CHAPTER 8	The Public Relations World
CHAPTER 9	That (So-Called) "Good Job"
CHAPTER 10	The Freelancing Life
EPILOGUE	Stepping Out on Faith

"Good Job"

CHAPTER ONE

No More Tears (Moving Forward Despite the Fear)

I tell this story all the time when I'm speaking to journalism students or groups. I was 22 years old. I was preparing to leave Southern University with a degree in mass communication and become the first person in my family to graduate from college. I already had a job in my field. I was getting ready to move out of state to pursue my career. I was so excited. As the folks say, "You couldn't tell me nothing." Or my mother would say, "I was just *beside myself*."

I had gotten a paid internship at the *Grand Rapids Press* in Grand Rapids, Mich. Mind you, I didn't know a soul at the newspaper except my editor who I had only spoken to on the phone. Fortunately, I had a friend from college who was from Grand Rapids. He was still in school when I graduated, but he gave me the names of some of his friends and contacts. I was *so* ready to start my life. I was ready to leave my hometown of Baton Rouge and see the world. I was so eager that I had scheduled my move one week after graduation.

"Good Job"

So here's the scene: I'm getting dropped off at the Baton Rouge airport by my parents and other relatives. I was going to rent a furnished studio apartment in Grand Rapids, so I only had to pack my clothes. I wasn't even going to have a car. Can you believe that? So my family and I said our goodbyes. I boarded the plane. The door shut and the plane started to take off. Then it hit me. I was leaving the comforts of home—a place where I had grown up—and was moving hundreds of miles away from my family. I was going to a strange land. I didn't know anyone. I was going to be alone. A fear came over me like I had never felt before. I started to cry and I couldn't stop. The flight attendant kept asking me if I was all right, and through big gulps of breath, I said, "Yes, I'm okay." The reality was that I was scared to death. I asked myself, "What was I *thinking*? What am I doing? What if it doesn't work out? What if I hate the job? What if I can't be a journalist? What if something bad happens to me? How am I going to be able to do this on my own? What makes me think I can have a career?" Self-doubt raised its ugly head. It was trying to talk me out of something that I really wanted. Luckily I couldn't just get off the plane, so a few hours later I arrived in Grand Rapids. Fortunately by then, I didn't have any more tears left. I wiped my face and never looked back.

"Good Job"

I started a job that I absolutely loved. I met new friends. I had the time of my life. It was one of the best decisions I have ever made. It laid the foundation for what was ahead—an exciting journalism career, not just a job.

Now, I could have turned around. I could have called my parents and gotten on the next flight back to Louisiana, but I didn't. I moved forward, felt the fear, and went ahead with my plans. What I learned has served me well all these years.

The Lesson: Don't ever let fear keep you away from your goals. Fear is a natural emotion. It's okay to feel fearful, but move forward *in spite* of it. You'll be glad you did. I know people who allow fear to keep them in dead-end jobs and loveless marriages or unhealthy relationships because they are afraid of the unknown. As they say, "At least this is the devil I know."

But know that everyone is afraid sometimes. Your manager is scared. Your spouse or partner is scared. Your parents are scared. I would even say the President of the United States gets scared because he's only human. None of us know if we're making the right decisions.

"Good Job"

Everyone is fearful of the unknown. Everyone is hesitant to change. I've made many changes in my career and my life, and change still is not easy for me. That's because there are no guarantees in life. You take a new job thinking it might be better than the old job, and you might find yourself facing even worse conditions. You start a new relationship with promise and for some reason, things just don't work out. That's life. That's the risk you take in moving forward. It's the cost of doing business, as they say, and ultimately becoming successful in life. Show me a person who is successful and I'll show you somebody who has taken many risks—some that worked out, some that didn't.

But know that the risk is worth taking each and every time, even if it doesn't work out. It makes you stronger. It makes you more knowledgeable, and aware of what you don't want. That's the first step to getting what you really want.

And often, when you take that first step, you'll find that everything else falls in place. It certainly did for me in Grand Rapids, as taking that risk laid the foundation for a wonderful journalism career that has been more exciting than I ever could have thought or imagined.

"Good Job"

CHAPTER TWO

The Right Attitude

Travel back in time with me to Michigan. I was a paid intern working as a general assignment reporter for the *Grand Rapids Press*. I was living my dream. I was exactly where I wanted to be—working in my field and doing what I wanted to do. I was living on my own in a furnished studio apartment. I made new friends. I experienced new things.

Life was great. The job was great. My editors were very supportive, as was the rest of the staff. I got to cover everything from festivals to conferences to the Army's Golden Knights parachute team, even flying with them while they jumped out of the side of the plane. I got sick, by the way, but it was still a thrill.

I was interning along with other students from Michigan State University and the University of Michigan. I was eager to learn, taking full advantage of this great opportunity to hone my journalism skills.

In other words, I had the right attitude. What I lacked in skills I made up for with my enthusiasm and hard work. I was always willing to go on assignments and loved just hanging out in the newsroom, trying to soak up

"Good Job"

everything that I could. I loved seeing my byline—my name printed above my articles in the newspaper.

Management took notice. Although my internship was supposed to last three months, it ended up lasting longer. When my time was up, my editor helped me find my next job. I remember him saying to me that I wasn't yet ready to work for the paper full-time. He felt I needed to develop my skills a little more, and there was a smaller paper that was part of the same media company that would be a good fit for me. He put in a good word for me, which resulted in me landing an interview and then the job.

That job was at the *Muskegon Chronicle* in Muskegon, Mich., about 40 miles from Grand Rapids. It was a much smaller paper. I interviewed on a Friday and literally moved to Muskegon over the weekend. Talk about quick! The job was great. I was blessed with great editors and colleagues who treated me well. They were very supportive and seemed happy to have me. In return, I was ecstatic to be there. I tried to learn as much as I could. I tell people all the time that my reporting jobs at the *Grand Rapid Press* and the *Muskegon Chronicle* were two of the best jobs I've ever had. Everything was right. Management was great. My assignments were awesome. My coworkers were cool. It was the ideal situation.

"Good Job"

My editors would send me notes, telling me how much they enjoyed my articles and how glad they were to have me as part of the team. Later in my career, I realized just how special my experience in Michigan was.

The Lesson: Always work hard. Always have a positive attitude. It will serve you well. Smile, be helpful, be curious, and do more than what's expected.

Learning the technical skills is part of your on-the-job training. Having a great attitude is something that we can all bring with us.

"Good Job"

CHAPTER THREE

The Right Place at the Right Time

I had been in Muskegon about a year. I was working as a general assignment reporter and education reporter, covering school board meetings and the school district in the Muskegon area.

I came up with the idea to cover this story in Chicago about multicultural education. At the time, it was a new trend to include a variety of cultures in the curriculum.

I pitched it to my bosses. They liked the idea, so I traveled to Chicago on assignment. I was so excited to be living my dream –writing, reporting, and traveling. I was going to the "big city."

I took a cab to my hotel in downtown Chicago, which happened to be next door to Johnson Publishing Company, the home of *EBONY* and *JET* magazines and Fashion Fair Cosmetics. JPC, as it was called, was the media and cosmetics company founded and owned by John H. Johnson, a pioneering African-American entrepreneur. The magazines were among the first to celebrate Black life. I remember seeing *EBONY* and *JET* on the coffee tables at homes throughout the Black community when I was growing up.

"Good Job"

I arrived at my hotel and got out of the cab. A friendly guy walked by, and asked me if he could help me with my luggage. Being naïve, I said yes. Ron and I started talking, and discovered that we had a lot in common. He worked at Johnson Publishing Company and was a graduate of Grambling State University in Louisiana. As you might know, my *alma mater* Southern University and Grambling are longtime rivalries that play each other on national TV during the annual big Bayou Classic Game in New Orleans. Ron and I ended up having dinner and talking about our careers. I casually mentioned that I'd love to work at *EBONY* or *JET* one day. At the time, mind you, I was very happy at the *Muskegon Chronicle* and had no intention of going anywhere.

When I got back to Michigan, Ron called me and said he'd mentioned me to his bosses. He asked me to send a resume because there was an opening in JPC's public relations and marketing department, which was responsible for promoting the magazines and other happenings at the company.

I was flattered—so I sent Ron my resume, thinking at the very least I'd get a trip back to Chicago. I certainly wasn't interested in another job. It turns out the manager was interested in *me*, so I was invited for an interview. I was

"Good Job"

thinking, "Why not? It would be a great experience." As the saying goes, "Be careful what you ask for."

The interview was a memorable one, as I actually interviewed with the legendary Mr. Johnson. He was a no-nonsense kind of guy. He asked me, "What will it take to get you here?" It's a question you dream of getting asked when you're interviewing for a job. Of course I was young and naïve, and really didn't know how to answer the question. I said something to the effect of, "I just want a good salary that's comparable to living in Chicago." Ask me that question now. I'd offer a lot more specifics, like lots of vacation time, stock options, a signing bonus, and much more.

Mr. Johnson said okay, and that was that. I have to pause here for a moment to tell you what a great person he was. Mr. Johnson was very kind to me. But make no mistake about it, he also was a shrewd businessman. I say that with the utmost respect for the things he accomplished—especially during the times he accomplished them. One of the highlights of my career was working for him and getting to know him.

After the interview, I went back to Muskegon. Little did I know that my life was about to change dramatically.

The Lesson: Don't be afraid to wander outside of your comfort zone and always be open to chance meetings. They can alter your life in a big

"Good Job"

way. You never know who you might meet or who will change your life. It's happened over and over again for me.

Also, don't be afraid to tell people what you want or what you'd like to do one day. If I had never mentioned my desire to work for Johnson Publishing Company, I don't know if I would have ever gotten the chance.

"Good Job"

CHAPTER FOUR

Making the Right Decision

When I returned to work in Muskegon, I gave a lot of thought to the question of what I'd say if JPC offered me the job.

Initially, I decided that I wouldn't take it. I didn't want to work in public relations. I was a journalist at heart. I had a great job already. I felt supported and respected and I had a lot of flexibility.

The manager at Johnson Publishing Company called me. She said, "We hired someone else for the job that you interviewed for, but we want to offer you a job at *JET* magazine as a writer." Wait! Whoa! What?

I had been prepared to say "thanks, but no thanks" to the PR job. This was *totally* different. It was almost too good to be true. I was going to be writing for a national magazine in one of the largest cities in the nation. I was confused, flattered, and very excited. I didn't know what to do. I told the JPC manager I needed to think about it and get back to her. I called friends and relatives to tell them about my dilemma. They told me I needed to pray about it and follow my heart.

I even talked with my editor at the paper. He told me that he'd hate to see me leave, but I could always come back if it didn't work out. That sealed the

"Good Job"

deal for me. Previously, I was torn because I felt a great deal of loyalty to the paper for the way they treated me. I didn't want to just jump ship. However, after he told me that, I felt like it was okay to leave.

I called the manager back, telling her that I wanted to come back and interview for the job. She said they weren't going to fly me back to Chicago, but Mr. Johnson would call me and answer all my questions.

Here's our conversation as I recall it:

"Hi, Mr. Johnson," I said.

"Hello," he said.

"I have a few questions."

"Okay."

"What about the benefits?"

"Oh, we have medical benefits just like the ones you have there."

"What exactly will I be doing?"

"You will be covering stories like you do there."

These questions-and-answers went on for a few more minutes.

Then he said something to the effect of, "Do you want the job or not?"

"Yes!"

"Good Job"

Hilarious and classic Mr. Johnson. To the point. No nonsense. I was headed to the Windy City.

The Lesson: Be open to change, even if it's not part of your plan. You never know what life holds for you. I hadn't planned on taking the job, but I'm certainly glad I did. The great thing about life is that you don't have to stick to the plan. It's *your* plan. You can change it at any time! Also, take advantage of opportunities that come your way. They don't come often—and might not come again—so sometimes you just have to go for it.

"Good Job"

CHAPTER FIVE

Living in the Big City

I arrived in Chicago—the Windy City. I was working as an assistant editor, writing national stories for an historic publication. I was living the dream. *JET* was an amazing place—and felt like a living history museum. Some of my editors and colleagues had been there since the magazine was founded in the 1950s. I was part of the staff that wrote and edited stories for the magazine. *JET* was a weekly publication, so we had weekly deadlines. We wrote and rewrote a lot of stories, all of which covered the Black community across the nation.

Some of the highlights of my career was meeting Civil Rights icon Rosa Parks, singers Jermaine and Randy Jackson, and NBA great Michael Jordan (I was living in Chicago when the Bulls won their first three championships). I interviewed actress Lela Rochon (of "Waiting to Exhale" fame) and R&B singer Anita Baker. I also met Oprah Winfrey (I had a chance to attend the taping of one of her "Oprah" talk shows) and her longtime boyfriend Stedman Graham.

"Good Job"

I enjoyed working at *JET* and being part of the staff. My colleagues were funny and personable. It was like a family. Working for *JET* opened a lot of doors for me in the city. The company was well-respected. I remember going to all the concerts and other big events happening around town, thanks to where I worked.

Another perk of working at *JET*: the cheap eats. The company served lunch in the cafeteria for only $1 a day. It was like having dinner at lunch every day—fish, spaghetti, salad, dessert, and a drink. All for $1. Mr. Johnson would also host parties for celebrities on the top floor. While I didn't get to go to all of them, the stars would be escorted around the office so I'd at least get to meet them.

Socially, it was a great job. However, after two years, I decided that I wanted to do more. I resigned my position and changed careers.

The Lesson: Enjoy the ride. Take it all in. Every experience leads you to the next. Learn as much as you can and continue moving forward.

"Good Job"

CHAPTER SIX

Changing Course

After *JET*, I went to work for Amoco Corporation, which is now BP. I'd met the folks at Amoco while working on a story for *JET*. Turns out Mr. Johnson and Amoco Corporation had a long history together when the company was called Standard Oil. I was sent to do a story on the company, and that's how I met their public relations staff. When I got ready to move into PR, I talked with them as well as lots of other folks.

Let me back up here. I am a true journalist. Before I dive into something, I research it. I talk to people who are doing what I'd like to do. This is what's called "informational interviewing." Because I wanted to explore careers in public relations, I'd call someone that I met at a reception—or even "cold call" them without an introduction. I may have read about the person in the newspaper, or perhaps saw them on TV. When I'd call, I'd tell them who I was and ask if I could come and talk with them about their job, because I was thinking about making the transition to public relations. I made sure to point out that I wasn't necessarily looking for a job—I just wanted information. Most people said yes. Some didn't. Some talked to me over the

"Good Job"

phone. Some met with me in person. I talked to public relations managers in corporations and account executives at PR agencies. I wanted to get a feel for the variety of jobs that were available.

It helped me figure out what kind of public relations job I wanted—whether I wanted to work in a PR agency or corporate America. I eventually decided I wanted to do corporate public relations. It seemed to fit my personality best. I liked structure. I knew I liked working for a big company, and all the perks and resources that came with that. I also enjoyed traveling.

After a couple of months of research, I started looking for a full-time job. I called the guy that I'd met at Amoco to see if there were any opportunities. One was available, so I sent my resume and eventually got a job based in Chicago. Here's something interesting. At the time I was hired at Amoco, the company was going through some major layoffs. I learned a valuable lesson. Companies often still hire despite laying other people off, so don't be discouraged if the company is going through some changes. It's the natural flow of things.

The man who was responsible for hiring me knew my editor at the *Grand Rapids Press*. They'd gone to college together. Small world, isn't it? He called my former editor, who thought I could do no wrong and he gave his friend at Amoco a glowing review of me. I think that's a big part of the

"Good Job"

reason that I got the job. After all, it's not what you know, but *who* you know. I do believe that is true to a large degree.

The Lesson: The world is really small. I know it sometimes seems enormous, but after you've worked a couple of places, you'll discover it's extremely tight and closely connected. Always do your best. Try to leave your last employer on good terms. In other words, don't burn bridges.

Also, don't be afraid to switch gears. I'm asked all the time about how to make the transition from one area to another. It's a process. Everything starts with a plan.

Remember, you can always go back (to what you were doing before, albeit a different company) if it doesn't work out. And sometimes, you can return to your previous employer! Nothing is etched in stone. The great thing about life is that *it's your life*. You can change it whenever you like.

"Good Job"

CHAPTER SEVEN

Corporate America

I was now working for a very large company with offices around the world. I was a writer for the Amoco company newspaper, covering news around the company much like I had covered the education beat for the *Muskegon Chronicle*. I got to travel and meet people at all levels of the company, from junior staff members to head honchos. It was a fun job, and I enjoyed it. I liked working in the Amoco building, a high rise in downtown Chicago with restaurants and coffee shops on the first floor. I really felt like I was really living the big-city life, as I lived and worked downtown.

After a couple of years working on the Amoco newspaper staff, I wanted to do something else. I'm always looking to expand and grow. That's really been my motto. There were always a number of public relations positions available within the company at various locations. I'd decided that the next time one of those jobs came open, I'd apply.

The next job happened to be in Houston. At the time, I had no plans to ever leave Chicago. I loved living in Chi-town, even though it was a little cold for a girl from the South. I really thought I'd retire there, but I applied for

"Good Job"

the job in Houston because I wanted my bosses to know that I was interested in moving on to bigger and better things.

The job opportunity was located at Amoco's offices in Houston. It was a public affairs job working with the exploration and production offices and servicing internal clients, in addition to writing for the company's internal newspapers and magazines. I was invited for an interview and flew to Houston to meet with my potential bosses.

Once I got to Houston, I was hooked. I loved the job responsibilities. I loved where the offices were located. I enjoyed talking with my future boss and coworkers. Next thing I knew, I was packed and on my way to Houston.

The Lesson: Let your bosses know that you are interested in other opportunities. Apply for positions. Ask to be considered for the job. You will never move up if you don't ask.

"Good Job"

CHAPTER EIGHT

The Public Relations World

I loved Houston. I still love Houston. It was another big city like Chicago, but the weather was warm and it was closer to my hometown. I enjoyed working with internal clients locally, as well as in places such as Tulsa, Okla. My job involved a lot of writing, editing, interacting with the community, attending community events, and working with the schools. It was really a fun job. I met some good friends and colleagues while there. The offices were nice and were located at Westlake, with an actual lake adjacent to the various office buildings.

I had my own office, which I loved. It was challenging work that allowed me to grow in a variety of ways. I also learned a lot about the oil and gas industry.

I stayed in this position for about five years, and then got a job at Amoco's Texas City refinery. I was doing the same job: writing, editing, representing the company at various functions, and serving as a company spokesperson. I also hosted a TV show that was broadcast within the refinery. That's when the TV bug started biting … but more on that later.

"Good Job"

I enjoyed working at the refinery, and enjoyed my colleagues. It was a two-person Public Affairs shop—just my boss and me—so I had a lot of autonomy. The work was challenging in a fun kind of way.

I wrote and edited a magazine. The work seemed to be combination of all the things I had done so far.

However, after about two years or so on the job, I began to get restless. I was tired of writing about refinery equipment and technology. I wanted to cover fun stories again, so I started freelancing for the local newspaper. I'd write stories for $50 an article about something that was going on in the community, whether it was an event happening at a school or a profile about someone doing something interesting.

Once again, I did my research. I knew some people who were freelance writers, so I talked to them and I cold-called people to ask them for information. That's how I found out that the local paper hired freelancers. I loved writing freelance pieces about what was happening in the community so much so that I'd sometimes write my articles at work.

The reality was that I missed journalism. I really am a journalist at heart, and I missed writing stories and reporting in a journalistic way. Once I saw

"Good Job" my byline again, I got excited all over again. The rush returned. I knew that I had to find a way to return to my first love full-time.

The Lesson: If you're not enjoying your job anymore, you should do something else. You're not doing yourself or your bosses any favors by staying somewhere you don't want to be. Believe me, it shows—even if you try your best to hide it. Find something you're passionate about and go for it. Life is short—try to make the most of it.

Do your research. Talk to people who are doing what you want to do. People love to talk about themselves, so take advantage of that fact and pick their brains.

"Good Job"

CHAPTER NINE

That (So-Called) "Good Job"

I had been thinking about quitting my public affairs job. I was freelancing while I was working on my plan to leave Amoco. I wanted to go back to being a journalist.

I wrote it down in my journal. I put everything on paper, as things seem more real when you put write them down. I was trying to figure out the right time to leave my job.

It was a job that all my family and friends kept telling me was a "good job." And it was. The pay was good and the benefits were great. But my friend Maureen told me something that I will never forget: "It's not a good job if it's not a good job for YOU."

But I didn't know what I wanted to do next. I didn't know whether to go back to writing for newspapers or magazines, or try my hand at television. I had been thinking about a career in TV for a while. I'd watch the news and say to myself, *"I can do that."* I thought it would be fun.

So I just kept putting off making a decision. I was thinking and thinking about what I wanted to do and how I would do it. Then my godmother—

"Good Job"

who was like a second mom to me—got sick. *Really* sick. I had to travel home to Baton Rouge to help take care of her. I was going there quite a bit, and it was a struggle to keep up with everything on the job, while trying to be there for my family.

I remember thinking one day, "Why am I rushing to go back to a job I don't really enjoy anymore, and leaving someone I love who really needs me *now*?" I knew right then and there that I had to quit my job so I could spend time with my godmother. I was going to quit, anyway. This just moved the timetable up a bit.

So I resigned. My plan was to take care of my godmother, and then start my full-time freelancing career.

This was not an off-the-cuff decision. As I said, I had been thinking about quitting for a while. And I had taken steps to be in a good financial position to allow myself some time off.

When I shared the news with family and some of my friends, they thought I was crazy. All I heard was, "Why are you quitting that 'good job?' A lot of people would love to have that 'good job.' How are you going to support yourself freelancing? What *is* freelancing, anyway?"

I knew their concerns were legitimate because they loved me, and they wanted to make sure I was going to be okay. But you can let others' doubts

"Good Job"

throw you off of your plan if you're not careful. They will have you second-guessing your decision, but you have to be strong and stay focused.

I knew that this was what I wanted to do, so I explained to them very briefly what was going on. I told them, "This is what I want to do. I have a plan, and I'm going to be fine. I appreciate your concerns, but the decision has already been made and I'm happy about it.'"

I think my positivity put them at ease, and it allowed me to move forward without answering a million other questions.

The Lesson: Follow your own heart. It's your life. Not your mama's. Not your daddy's. Not your kids'. It's YOURS. Do what you want to do. Do what makes you happy. Don't let others talk you out of your dreams. I've never regretted leaving my job to take care of my godmother and become a freelance writer. In fact, it's one of my proudest decisions!

"Good Job"

CHAPTER TEN

The Freelancing Life

I spent about a month helping to take care of my godmother. Then my plan was to start my freelance career full-time. I thought if I had more time to write, I could make more money. Like a good journalist, I did my research. I talked to friends, colleagues, and people I didn't know to find out how they made it work, and which publications hired freelancers. I got a feel for what freelancers could charge for their work.

I learned that one of my favorite magazines of all time, *People*, hired freelancers. So the first thing I did was contact the editors at the magazine and tell them I was interested in working for them.

I had several things going for me. I'd worked as a journalist for newspapers and other magazines. I was able to show recent examples of my work because I'd freelanced for the local paper. And most important, I was available because I was currently unemployed—or rather, newly *self-employed*.

People hired me right away. My first assignment was to interview the judge who was presiding over President Bill Clinton's impeachment proceedings after his alleged affair with intern Monica Lewinsky. The judge was from

"Good Job"

Lake Charles, La., which was right up the road from Baton Rouge on Interstate 10.

My editor sent me there to find out everything I could about this judge. The great thing about reading the magazine is that you find out lots of interesting tidbits about the person being profiled—how they grew up, their special memories, their likes and dislikes.

I tracked down some of the judge's childhood friends through friends of mine, and by asking around, meeting people, and telling them who I was and what I was doing. I'd hit the jackpot. It was exactly what the editors wanted. That led to many other assignments with *People*. Some of my biggest stories included covering the horrific dragging death of James Byrd, Jr. in Jasper, Texas; the June 1999 plane crash in Little Rock, Ark.; interviewing Beyoncé when Destiny's Child was going through lineup changes, and hanging out in Dallas with Bishop T.D. Jakes of the Potter's House, where NFL legends Deion Sanders and Emmitt Smith were members. One of my all-time favorite assignments was covering San Antonio Spurs star Sean Elliott's return to basketball after he received a donated kidney from his brother. I got to go to a Spurs game (and had floor seats!), hang out with Sean at his house, and conduct interviews in the

"Good Job"

locker room. I also covered the tragic deaths of the five children in Houston who were drowned by their mother, Andrea Yates. I covered the funeral, and also wrote an article for CNN.com.

Writing for *People* was a great gig. I really enjoyed the travel and the perks that came with writing for the magazine. I worked with good local editors, as well as those in New York City.

I also freelanced for *Time* magazine, *O The Oprah* Magazine, *Essence*, *Emerge* (where I wrote a cover story on James Byrd's family)*,* the *Houston Chronicle*, and the *Washington Post.*

Another all-time favorite assignment was writing for Oprah's magazine. I had been pitching articles to an *O* editor, but hadn't had any success. Then one Saturday, I was attending a meeting of women in the media in Houston where the guest speaker was a woman who was a sketch artist for the Houston Police Department. Her story was fascinating because although she was helping rape victims and others find their perpetrators, she had been raped years earlier, but never reported it. So by helping others, she was also helping herself to heal. I knew this story had *O* written all over it.

One of the keys to successful freelancing is knowing what kinds of stories to pitch to which magazines. You have to understand the publication inside and out.

"Good Job"

After getting the sketch artist's contact information that afternoon, I raced home and sent an e-mail pitching the story to an *O* editor. She replied immediately that she was interested. She told me she wanted a 1,500-word article—and how much the magazine would pay for it. She asked *me* when I could get it to her. After hearing what they paid, I thought to myself, "For that fee, I could get it to you *tonight*." I submitted the article a few days later. My friends in Houston threw a party in my honor to celebrate my first article in *O*.

People ask me all the time—what's the key to a successful freelancing career? I freelanced full-time for nearly three years, and bought my first home during that time. The key is being aggressive—and always being available to current and potential clients.

For instance, *People* was divided into regions, and during the time I wrote for the region that included Oklahoma, Texas, Louisiana, and other states. If any news stories broke those areas, I knew the editors would need to send someone to cover it—so I made sure I was the first freelancer to call and let them know I was available. I'd watch the news or read the paper religiously, and if there was breaking news in those areas, I'd immediately get on the phone.

"Good Job"

The other thing that worked for me is that I could stay on the story as long as needed. I was available to them 24/7, because this was my full-time job. Flexibility is the key when it comes to freelancing. I needed to be available for my editors when they called me to cover a story, and I needed to be flexible enough to follow through and get the story done—no matter how long it took.

But full-time freelancing isn't for everyone. You're working for yourself, so when you don't have an assignment, you don't get paid. You have to get used to the financial rollercoaster that comes along with this lifestyle. One month, you could be very busy. The next month, no one might call. The key to offsetting this problem is finding a client you can work for on a regular basis, which is what I was able to do with *People*.

Freelancing is like having your own small business. That comes with perks—the flexibility of working at home in your pajamas and traveling to cover a story—and the not-so-good challenges of up-and-down earnings and having to pay for your own health insurance.

The other key to freelance writing is developing a keen understanding of publications and their areas of focus. In addition to getting called on assignment for breaking news stories, I also had to pitch, or propose, stories. That means calling editors and trying to convince them to pay me to cover

"Good Job"

the story idea that I am proposing. In order to do this successfully, you must understand the kinds of stories that publication covers. You do this by reading the publication and becoming very familiar with the stories they print and publish. You can also do this by asking editors which type of stories interest them and their readers.

For instance, *O The Oprah Magazine* regularly published stories about women's lives that featured a spiritual or deep connection. I loved reading *O*, so when I heard the Houston Police Department sketch artist woman speak, I immediately knew her story would appeal to its editors. As I learned that day, a good story sells itself.

Just as is true in life, successful freelancing is about establishing good relationships—and in my case, relationships with editors at the publications for which I wanted to write. I also targeted magazines that I enjoyed reading because I already belonged to their target audiences.

The Lesson: Freelancing is not for everyone, but if you're comfortable living a little on the edge—and if you're aggressive—you can make it work.

Also, dream big. I never thought I'd write for such noted publications as *People* Magazine, but I did my homework and good things happened.

"Good Job"

EPILOGUE

Stepping Out on Faith

I've taken many risks in my career. Some didn't pay off, but I'm happy to say most of them did.

Don't be afraid to step out on faith. I had no idea what my life would be like when I moved across the country as a 22-year-old college grad. I had no idea things would work out as well as they did.

But I stepped out on faith, knowing that with God in my corner, I couldn't help but succeed.

I encourage you to do the same. Take chances, and if they don't work out, do something else. Life is all about making adjustments. It's like sports. When teams don't perform well in the first half, their coaches make adjustments and their teams come back stronger in the second half.

You have to think to yourself: "What is the worst that can happen?" As long as you're okay with the answer, move forward. Believe me, it's definitely worth it.

"Good Job"

I wrote this book about my personal journey in hopes of inspiring you to begin—or continue—pursuing *your* dreams. I really believe it's never too late to get started.

Throughout these 10 chapters, I've shared Lessons I've learned along the way. Some additional final thoughts as you pursue your destiny:

1. Move forward despite the fear. Don't let fear keep you stuck.

2. People are quick to tell you "no," but don't let that be the final word. A friend of mine says, "No means know." It means the person needs to know more in order to give you what you want.

3. Remember, it's not a good job if it's not a good job for YOU. You're the one who has to go to work every day.

4. Listen to yourself. Sure, it's great to get advice from others. In fact, I recommend seeking out others' opinions or expertise. But at the end of the day, you have to do what's best for you. And only *you* know what's best for you. Trust your own instincts.

"Good Job"

5. Don't get caught up in living someone else's life. Do what you want. It's *your* life, and you only get to live it once.

6. Don't let mistakes sideline you. We all make mistakes. Learn from your mistakes and move on. It's the only way to grow.

7. Tell people what you want. They can't help you if they don't know what you want. Share your dreams and desires. You'll be surprised what happens when you do.

8. Don't be afraid to ask for what you want. You may not get it, but you definitely *won't* if you don't ask.

9. Be persistent. All you need is one 'yes.'

10. Life is short, so enjoy the ride. Find something you enjoy doing, and find a way to get paid for it. Then every paycheck will feel like a bonus.

# # #

CPSIA information can be obtained
at www.ICGtesting.com
Printed in the USA
LVIC06n2147090714
393677LV00002B/9